SUDDENLY
SCHOOLING

SUDDENLY SCHOOLING

A Survival Guide for Panicky Parents

 ACOMA PRESS

Catherine L. Morgan

Suddenly Schooling: A Survival Guide for Panicky Parents

Copyright © 2020 by Catherine L. Morgan

Published 2020 by Acoma Press

Portions of this work have appeared on Catherine Morgan's blog, www.catherinesletters.com.

Unless otherwise noted, all Bible references are from the ESV® Bible (The Holy Bible, English Standard Version®), copyright © 2001 by Crossway, a publishing ministry of Good News Publishers. Used by permission. All rights reserved.

Requests for information should be addressed to:

Acoma Press
40 W. Littleton Blvd. Suite 210, PMB 215
Littleton, CO 80120

www.acomapress.org
info@acomapress.org

Cover Design & Interior Layout: Evan Skelton

First Printing, 2020

Printed in the United States of America

Paperback: 978-1-7354826-4-4
PDF: 978-1-7354826-5-1

Cultivate wonder in your children, make your home a chapel of praise. Give thanks, always, with a glad heart. Look for God's fingerprints. Treasure God's Word. Treasure each other. Live for eternity.

Catherine L. Morgan,
Thirty Thousand Days

CONTENTS

INTRODUCTION

On a number of memorable occasions, the history of the world has taken a sudden, dramatic U-turn when calamity struck. Sometimes disastrously—Pompeii comes to mind. But sometimes catastrophe leads to an unexpectedly happy ending:

A wrong turn leads to the discovery of a continent (happy for the explorers: not, perhaps, so happy for the inhabitants of said continent).

A battle disastrously lost rallies the losing side to fight all the harder, turning the tide of the war. (Think Pearl Harbor.)

The discovery of cheese. (Whoever decided to transport milk in a sheep's stomach is high on my list of personal heroes.)

COVID-19 and the ensuing tidal wave of cultural and economic fallout will affect every sphere of our society in ways unimaginable, unpredictable even now. Wearing masks to the grocery store? No big deal. The widespread cancellation of public schools? Huge, hairy deal.

Suddenly, parents around the world must weigh the potential consequences of allowing children out in public against the potential consequences of keeping them home—not for a stray sick day, but for an entire grade. For many, there's not even a choice: your neighborhood school simply isn't physically open for business this year, but has gone online. Parents for whom homeschooling was unthinkable are reluctantly strapping in for a year of home-based education. You can spot these parents by their panicked, disheveled look—wild-eyed, hair standing on end, like the burglars who ran into Kevin McCallister in *Home Alone*. They never saw it coming.

But perhaps the year ahead of us is less of an unmitigated catastrophe and more of a happy accident. Perhaps it is a year of unprecedented opportunity.

For those who did not anticipate homeschooling, I can relate. My first two children, born 20 months apart, toddled off to our local charter school without incident. It was a great school—rigorous but not ridiculous, orderly but gentle, safe and fun. Up through the third grade, Joshua and Abigail dressed in matching uniforms and spent their days learning reading, writing, and arithmetic just a mile from home, while I cheerfully volunteered, tended the baby, and laid plans for the day when all three would be enrolled in school. But when our youngest, Patrick, entered preschool, we began to notice...anomalies. (FYI, he's given me permission to share what I'm about to say.)

Patrick was a unique kiddo. Bright as a button, but slower to pick up on certain skills. It gradually became apparent that he had special needs—sensory processing disorder, a different timetable for developmental milestones, off-the-charts intelligence coupled with some learning differences. As I sat in the back of our charter school's classrooms, I tried to imagine him there, pigeon-holed into the same learning sequence as everyone else. I couldn't imagine it. If I were to send this precocious, precious little guy off to the same school where my other two children thrived, I feared it would crush him.

And so, with a gulp, we decided to homeschool. Not just our youngest, but all three, reasoning that with this newfound freedom from schedules we could take epic field trips, giving all of our kids an opportunity for some outside-the-box learning.

For the past ten years we have been on the homeschool journey. Joshua and Abigail, previously a grade apart, I grouped into one "class." We've tried lots of things—two years completely on our own, multiple years in a public/homeschool hybrid co-op, a smattering of online classes, and, for the older kids, three years of an innovative public high school. I was, of course, terrified that in sending our older two back to public school I would learn just how much I'd fallen short as their teacher, but I needn't have worried. They jumped in with verve and didn't skip a beat. In fact, both snagged an associate's degree during high school. Patrick is just now entering high school, and though we expected to send him to public school, coronavirus came crashing into our plans.

Over the years, I've encountered many of the same obstacles looming before so many others. The cost-benefit analysis of making a major life decision. An unexpected transition. Kids who were used to one environment and had to adapt. Special needs. Different learning styles. Multi-stage children in a one room schoolhouse. Sorting through curriculum choices. Winging it. I understand very well the rising tide of panic, but as someone who is largely on the other side now, I marvel at the unforeseen blessings that rose from the ashes of my best-laid plans.

Breathe. God's got this. In fact, one day you might regard this season as the highlight of your parenting life.

1.

GRACE

Best guess? This pandemic will not last forever. Pandemics come and go, and our collective surprise at this one is not because it is unprecedented, but because we were unprepared. It seems reasonable to assume, with a dose of historical context, that this, too, shall pass. In all likelihood, the season of homeschooling which stretches before you will not be eternal; in another year or two, schools will reopen, teachers will return. Hopefully we'll be a little more cautious, a skosh more hygienic. Presumably, municipalities will think twice about overcrowding in the classroom, and measures will be taken to prevent contagion. But back to school they'll go, within this generation. Kids who've missed a year or two will once again dive into the dubious dodgeball arena and resume picking at underwhelming cafeteria food. Kids who (like two of mine) have the misfortune of missing all or part of their senior year, will nevertheless head off to college eventually. And there's the rub.

"What if?" we're all asking. "What if little Lily misses a year with her classmates and can never catch up? What if little Billy falls behind?" What if, what if, what if. Anxiety rises in the back of our throats like bile. It's easy to give in to fear.

May I suggest: take a deep breath.

There are a few salient facts which get lost in the chaos of panic.

Fact number one: we are all in the same boat.

Your kiddos are not the only ones whose lives have been upended. This will be part of the story they tell one day, how they survived the coronavirus years, how it changed them. There will be hard things that make them stronger. There will be sweet memories that grow up like wildflowers in the weeds.

When your children return to school, they will not be unusual. Teachers will have grace. Even colleges will cut them some slack. For that matter, the most prestigious colleges are currently fighting for survival, and admission standards will necessarily adapt. Perhaps algebra gets delayed a year. So what? Our kids may catch a lucky break here.

In the years following World War I, universities worldwide struggled to stay afloat. C.S. Lewis, one of the best-known Oxford dons of all time, was admitted to the university in spite of failing the prerequisite math exam. Had he applied to Oxford in peacetime, he may have been rejected.

I'm not suggesting we take a year-long vacation, but do remember that this isn't an ordinary year. The inherent opportunity hidden in this moment is a rare gift.

The fear of falling behind is laced with another, deeper fear, the fear of inadequacy. What if I'm not up to snuff for this homeschooling project?

Fact number two: there is no recipe for creating perfect children, and no foolproof plan for launching them into a perfect life.

Our desire to produce children on the upper end of the bell-shaped curve is rooted in twin sins—pride and shame. We want our children to be the best, better than others. We want them to reflect our brilliance in parenting. We want Gold Medal Winners. But because we know that we're not perfect, we fear that our kids will expose our weakness to the world. We'll fail as parents, so they'll fail as people.

There are a lot of flaws in this thinking: our arrogance, our grasping at success, our self-flagellation. If you could control every last detail of your child's daily life, could you guarantee the outcome? Only if she were not an individual with her own ideas and her own conscience. Only if parenting, and by extension, education, were a chemistry experiment.

Psychologist John B. Watson famously asserted, "Give me a dozen healthy infants, well-formed, and my own specified world to bring them up in and I'll guarantee to take any one at random and train him to become any type of specialist I might select—doctor, lawyer, artist, merchant-chief and, yes, even beggar-man and thief, regardless of his talents, penchants, tendencies, abilities, vocations and the race of his ancestors." The hubris of the man! Of his own four children, it is worth noting, three reportedly attempted suicide.

Yes, our children's education matters. Yes, we have enormous influence on our kids' lives, and responsibility to "train them up in the way they should go." No, we cannot by all of our strategies or perfect plans secure for our children a straight path to success.

It seems patently obvious to any veteran parent that we are just not in control. Obvious, maybe, but worth saying anyway. Some kids have to learn the hard way. Some kids are stubborn. Your idea of a perfect day and your child's are not going to always (or ever) line up. God's plan for an individual's life encompasses lessons learned and circumstances born out of tragedy, misfortune, self-discipline, and (supposed) serendipity. This year? The one with all of the potholes? God saw it coming. It was always part of the plan.

We know these things: that we're all in the same boat, that we're not in control. And yet we react as if good parents know what to do when a pandemic upends their plans. As if our local school has the secret sauce and all of our cupboards are bare. There is a tiny grain of truth here—some people are more naturally suited to teaching, just as some people are more naturally suited to parenting in general. I'd rather have Mr. Rogers for a dad, or a teacher, than, say, Mussolini. But if a loving, determined, reasonably intelligent adult wants to guide a pint-sized person through a year of school, it is certainly possible to do that well, even without a teacher's disposition or a grad school degree in education.

Fact number three: the basic ingredients of a great education are at your fingertips.

For one thing, you yourself presumably went through many years of school. You have seen teaching done well, and, probably, done poorly. You have a few decades more life experience than your child. You have a bundle of talents, strengths, and passions unique to you (and other things you'd just as soon avoid). You know your child better than almost anyone else on the planet could—how he thinks, what drives him, what hurdles he has to overcome. You probably have access to the internet. You probably live near a local library, a state park, a farm or a museum, a theater or a landmark. While you may not be naturally suited to teaching, you are quite capable of learning new things yourself every day. Could you not come alongside your child and learn with him?

Grace. We need it like we need water; without it we perish. Have grace on yourself. You are not perfect, but you are full of possibility. Sure, someone else might outdo you in demonstrating scientific principles with vinegar and baking soda. But maybe you are a stone cold math genius. Maybe you never got around to reading the classics, but now's your chance. Maybe you've always wished you had time to teach your kid to play the piano, or bake, or do jujitsu.

Maybe you'd like to read through a chunk of the New Testament out loud with your kids, but you worry that you don't have all the answers. Well, could you ask the questions? Could you say to your child, "Honey, I don't know. Let's look it up together"?

What if this year, though unconventional, turned out to be a magical moment in your kiddo's education—the year without worksheets, the year a book made her cry, the year you both saw something that took your breath away?

Your children need grace, too, a commodity in short supply in many classrooms. This year might be the first time in a long while that your children don't have to compete with their neighbor across the aisle. Homeschool might be a breath of fresh air for a child who's competitive or insecure. While you may not be able to give them the moon, you can surely give them grace.

Not to say giving grace is easy—by definition, grace is undeserved. There will be times when your patience is tested and you understand why the principal at your elementary school kept that paddle hanging on the wall. Many of the battles are predictable: one kid's hatred of math and another's of reading, the turning off of electronic devices, the getting out of bed. Having a game plan helps.

When we pulled our older two children out of school, I dreaded the uptick in complaining and bullheadedness that was sure to come. Our son, by the third grade, had such an unending pile of homework that from 3:00 until bedtime was turning into one long, protracted argument. How much harder would it be to teach them all day long? But to my great surprise, the temperature of our days immediately cooled when we began to homeschool. We worked hard, actually—I was no unschooler, and I'd chosen a fairly difficult curriculum. Still, I saw no need to swamp the kids with homework. When we were done, that was it—free time commenced until lights out. There was freedom. There was grace. Amazing.

All of us are feeling a little tender this year. The grief unleashed by successive waves of social turmoil and rampant sickness have taken a toll. The shock of social distancing has left millions of people feeling isolated and heartsick. We need to radically love one another, starting with those under our roof.

I don't know whether it's possible to quantify the emotional weight of the past year, but I know many of us are staggering under it. To extend to our children (and to ourselves) the gift of grace in myriad little ways—permission to rest, permission to lean into our strengths, laughter, forgiveness—is to lift the burden of grief just a little, to begin to heal.

Imagine a year of homeschooling free from the stress and guilt induced by the myth that you will screw up your kids' lives. Imagine you were given one year of significant freedom to invest in your kids' well-being and to dive into learning alongside them, taking advantage of blank calendars, your own circadian rhythms, your unique strengths, your intense insight into your kids' personalities, and the smorgasbord of educational resources we're privy to in this information age.

What if this calamity is a blessing in disguise?

2.

GIFT

One year of homeschool. Not what you expected. Not what you had planned. But what a gift it is! Let's explore three dimensions of the opportunity before you: the gift of relationship, the gift of discipleship, and the gift of rest. We'll come to the academic piece in the next section.

The Gift of Relationship

You would think that entire big box stores of time-saving devices would have bought us a lifetime of leisure and rest. We have washing machines to scrub our clothes and dryers to fluff them out again (in America, anyway. For some reason the British still make do with clotheslines.) We have Bluetooth, so that we can multi-task on the phone while we load the dishwasher, which will wash the dishes for us. We have instant access to Google (lest opening an encyclopedia is too much work). We have Alexa to pull up our favorite song and Amazon to deliver our groceries.

We have decluttered our closets, but not our lives.

We live in a world of scurry.

Our kids bop from Boy Scouts to Awana to soccer to piano. We have meetings on Monday nights, swim team on Tuesday nights, small group on Wednesday nights, youth group on Thursday nights. We welcome a constant barrage of pinging messages night and day—texts, emails, Facebook, Twitter.

There is rarely any quiet. There is rarely any rest.

A year of suddenly schooling, with all extracurriculars cancelled? The collective howl from all corners could create a sonic boom. Our kids (and their parents) are all activity junkies, and the idea of replacing wholesome exercise with more YouTube videos makes our skin crawl. Exchanging actual busyness with virtual busyness is no upgrade.

But what if we replaced any busyness with something richer?

What if we invested all of that extra time together to cultivate a new level of relationship?

This is one of those rare moments when we can hit pause and reevaluate. What are we aiming for? What's our vision for this family? How are our boundaries? What consumes our days? Are we tilting in any dangerous directions?

How are we loving one another?

Regardless of what curriculum you choose or how you schedule out your lesson plans (important things, but secondary), there are some big-picture questions that are begging to be considered. Taking time at the outset to reflect could make the difference between a year of miserable drudgery and a year of joyful discovery.

Remember that day when you first dropped off your kiddo for kindergarten? The lump in the throat as you realized how time flies? The minutes tick down until our kids leave home. This is it, our one shot to love, our one long road trip to make memories, to laugh, to raise up world-changers. How can we guard this treasure?

You might consider creating a family covenant to protect this bubble of time—not a bunch of rules handed down by management, but a team-building exercise. We did this ourselves a few years back, started with a study of some familiar Bible verses to set the tone, then created a love-saturated credo to help us aim high.[1] We never lived it out perfectly, but then, that's not the point. What was it Emerson said? "We aim above the mark to hit the mark."

Too often we aim for survival when joy is within reach.

The Gift of Discipleship

There are a great many things that we can outsource. We can hire a kid to mow the lawn, a woman to paint the walls, a tutor to explain the complexities of calculus. But one thing we never dare outsource is the discipleship of our children.

---

[1] See Appendix 1.

Many things compete for our kids' attention and allegiance: friends, worldviews, the cultural zeitgeist, social media, movies, books, teachers, homework, deadlines, Jimmy Fallon. The older they get, the less time they have, and the less our influence holds sway. Calculate for a moment what percentage of the day you spend speaking with your child. The rest of the time? Someone else is speaking to him.

Here is an unexpected opportunity to invest, hourly, in the spiritual well-being of your kids. In fact, you might make it a major goal of the school year.

I suggest we start by taking stock. Of ourselves. It's awfully hard to pass on what we don't possess. So how's my faith? How is my personal walk with Jesus? Devotional life? Prayer life? There's a list in Galatians of the "fruit of the Spirit": love, joy, peace, patience, kindness, goodness, faithfulness, gentleness, self-control.[2] Surely we each have an area we need to shore up. Ah, but we can't just pull ourselves up by our bootstraps and decide to be holy. Help!

---

[2] Galatians 5:22-23

If we haven't been in the habit of praying for the power of the Holy Spirit to invade and change us, now is a good time to start. We will certainly need an extra dose of that power to power through a year of unexpected homeschooling. Trust me.

And it's not about duty, it's about delight. I would contend that the "chief end" of parenting is to enjoy God, together, with our kids—to teach them, above all, to be amazed by grace. Which is more effective, a strict teacher with a posted list of rules and a table of facts, or a dazzling, delightful teacher who sweeps children up in the wonder of learning? The same principle applies to discipleship. Better by far to be dazzled by wonder and love than to strain for adherence to a bunch of commands.

I think it's also helpful to honestly take stock of our kids. Often it's easier for us to rattle off a list of someone's weaknesses than to describe their strengths. What if you made a long list of your kids' best qualities, and a very, very short list of areas that need improvement? Then scatter your speech with praise for what they do well—catch them in the act of goodness as often as possible. Conserve your energy, pick your battles carefully on the "room for improvement" list. Mostly? Pray. You can't fix your child, or even begin to change him, but God can.

Being a parent is not for the faint-hearted. You realize after a while that these little creatures are making plans, and they are not your plans. They are diving into danger with gusto and not much forethought, and pretty soon all the mamas are running full-tilt behind them, hollering out cautions and suggestions aplenty. We are raising little men and women, and they are rocketing into the future faster than we can rein them in.

These are the people who will shape the world.

You realize when you've been around the ring a time or two that most of the life-changing moments come down to your child and God. None of the steam you can produce from both ears, none of the dreams you've dreamed can alter the story written for him; your kid is on a journey you haven't scripted, making choices you would undo and letting the chips fall. Think of the long history of the world, the Jacobs and Esaus and Moseses, the Roosevelts and the Edisons and the MLKs. Think of all the mamas, running behind, waving a handkerchief vainly to keep them from boarding that train. Wouldn't you have cleaned up their stories a bit? Wouldn't you have wiped away the ugly parts? But then they'd never have become who they were, and our collective story wouldn't be what it is.

(If I were Mary, and I could somehow save my boy from his long, troubled road, I would, I would. But the nail that sank into his story turned out to be the fulcrum that levered the whole broken world out of the mess we were in. That ugly nail turned out to be grace.)

So how do we pray these kids into the people they are meant to be? What do we do when they're rushing headlong into disaster, or struggling in school, or driving us crazy?

There are a lot of squawks that sneak out before we get the hand over the mouth, a lot of late-night prayers. God give us the grace to hide our face in His shoulder and let Him do all the watching and worrying.

I find myself praying for grace a lot these days; praying for the grace to let go, the grace to be patient, the love to expect all things, believe all things, endure all things. I pray for faith in the Author and His perfectly beautiful story, and I remember all of the great men who started life as impetuous, not-always-wise boys. I pray for grace to put down what I'm doing and listen, really listen, whenever I can; for the first thing I say in the morning and the last thing I say at night to be sweet, and not overfull of finger-wagging.

Perhaps there are impossible hurdles ahead, but I remember that with our steadfast Father all things are possible.

We pray for our kids; we teach our kids to pray. We delight ourselves in the Lord; we teach our kids to walk in awe and wonder. Whatever faith you possess, share it, and watch it grow.

What's an aspect of your faith that you like to geek out about? Share that with your kids. Older kids? Dive into apologetics. Certainly a legit part of your school day could be a feisty conversation about evidence for the resurrection or a discussion of competing truth claims. Not your speed? Pick up a gripping missionary biography and read it aloud. Or maybe you're an artist. What if you did an art project illustrating the Psalms? All in all, it's probably best to keep it simple. Reading a chapter a day of the gospels and allowing time for leisurely conversation about the life of Christ could be the beginning of a lifelong habit, and have more impact in the long run than many more ambitious projects ever could.

If Christ is really the center of our lives, we won't relegate him to the margin of our days. "Delight yourself in the Lord, and he will give you the desires of your heart." (Psalm 37:4) Delight isn't on the clock, it's a constant.

The Gift of Rest

Imagine a child who has never lain back in the grass just to feel thin leaves whisper against his earlobe, never watched cloudplay to find a story told for him alone, never learned to hear the separate song of robin, sparrow, chickadee. How can he hear the loneliness of the owl-eyed little girl, the song of the skinny immigrant with his beautiful eyelashes, the dreams of the old lady, liver-spotted, with near 100 years of secrets, stories, songs?

How can a poverty of imagination purchase empathy?

Imagine a child who has never lain on the bedroom floor with *Peter Pan*, *Treasure Island*, *Hardy Boys*, never plucked out a tune on unfamiliar instruments, never learned to look for shooting stars.

How can he dream, who never dreams? How can he plan for tomorrow, who lives in the never-quiet racket of today? How can a poverty of thought purchase purpose?

Imagine a child nourished on binge-watching, blinking neon games, portable noise. There is no end to thumping bass and chime of inbox, the unceasing prattle of friends (no more waiting, even, for a phone call). There is no waiting, period. There is no delayed gratification, no longing, no patience needed. And we are surprised when impatience bears its ugly fruit.

We wonder why society seems always to be breaking down. We wonder why there are violent outbursts every day. Where is this carnage born? Is it a failure of legislation? Of health care? Of education? Of parenting? Or is it simply that we have forgotten how to sit, quiet?

It takes quiet to see—are you surprised? Sit for an hour in a nickel arcade and try to see your neighbor's heart, try to see your own. We have forgotten how to see what others see, forgotten how to slip into their shoes.

We have forgotten how to imagine, how to dream.

We have forgotten how to listen, how to wait.

We are always loud, forever moving. Why then are we surprised when there is no peace? We are paying for the sins of omission.

Without quiet, there is no thought.

Without thought, there is no thoughtfulness.

Without thoughtfulness, there is no empathy, no imagination, no vision.

Without vision, there is no reason for hope.

Without hope, there is no reason to live.

With nothing to lose, there are no inhibitions.

We sow the wind, and we shall reap the whirlwind (Hosea 8:7).

This year is an opportunity for emotional healing. It's a chance for your children to be still for a change, to look with fresh eyes at the world. It's a chance for rest—Sabbath, some might say—a pause in the never-ending pulse of the world. It's an opportunity to slow down, read more, gossip less, cease competing. Why not take this year as a gift, and let time, peace, and quiet, do their splendid work?

3.

TLWBAT

In college, I took a string of education courses. Truth be told, I've forgotten more than I remember, but one thing that stuck with me is an acronym: TLWBAT. The Learner Will Be Able To. For every activity we dreamed up, we were required to list out a string of specific, measurable objectives. Not facts to be learned, or rules to be memorized, but skills to be acquired.

The Learner Will Be Able To multiply by 7.

The Learner Will Be Able To contrast Lady Macbeth and her husband.

The Learner Will Be Able To make a grilled cheese sandwich.

Now, I think it's also a perfectly sound educational goal to say that The Learner Will *Know* x, y, or z, but the goal-setting exercise is sound. Identifying the purpose of any given educational activity is quite helpful. One quickly realizes that an activity with no purpose is pointless.

Over the years, I've set a handful of overarching academic goals for my kids, and aiming in that direction has given me vision, energy, and endurance:

I want my kids to be lifelong learners.

I want my kids to know how to think, not just what to think.

I want my kids to never lose their sense of wonder, their delight in God, or their love of neighbor.

I want my kids to grow in imagination, creativity, joy, and empathy.

I want my kids to pursue a meaningful vocation that taps into their unique personalities, talents, and passions.

Obviously, every activity is not created equal, and we spend time every day doing things that we simply have to do because they are required. (The Learner

Will Be Able To persevere without whining.) But having a vision for the next school year helps us thrive.

A year-long break from the traditional school routine is a year-long opportunity to try something new. For one year, your children won't have to do busy-work. There won't be any stalling because the bell's about to ring, or a week of state-mandated diagnostic tests, or trips to the locker, or visits from the guidance counselor. Imagine a school day stripped of all unnecessary time-sucks. It's quite possible to cover five subjects in five luxurious hours and then to be done for the day. You can start as late as 8:00 and still be done by 2:00, with an hour-long lunch break in the middle.

Did you just stop and count that out on your fingers? It doesn't seem possible, does it? Finished in five hours? But then you think, wait—five hours to fill??

Now before you have a panic attack, let's break it down.

Part of the day will involve you offering instruction or suggestions or direction of some kind, reading or demonstrating or even lecturing. Reading aloud is a surprisingly fun way to teach, and allows you to draw on others' expertise and thoughtful content.

For very small children, you'll be involved in 90% of their work, but the school day itself might be quite short. The older the child, the less your presence is required. Once you establish a rhythm and a trusted source of input (more on that later), you might have very little actual teaching to do at all.

Then what *will* Billy be doing? Part of the time, he'll be reading. Or watching an online course. Or writing. Or practicing the multiplication table with his sister. This is when you'll be in the next room, doing the bills, and occasionally checking in. I'd strongly encourage you *not* to print off giant packets of worksheets for the poor kid to do. Better by far to give him time creating, or reading. And there is so, so much good literature out there to peruse.

This is the perfect opportunity to go deep in a favorite subject, to spend copious amounts of time enjoying all of the classics, or to dive into multiple, integrated subjects in one fell swoop. Helping a child make connections between art, science, politics, religion, philosophy, and poetry will lead to lots of ah-ha moments.

The really great moments come when you can take a field trip bouncing off of your studies—difficult in a quarantining world, but not entirely impossible. A lot of the best cultural centers have come up with online tours, virtual reality walk-throughs, and streamed performances. Google Earth, for instance, has a stunning collection of resources, whereby your kids can explore the intersection of math and architecture, see the creatures of a coral reef, walk in the footsteps of Lewis and Clark, or stroll through the Taj Mahal (a bit disappointing compared to an actual flesh-and-blood visit, but quite accessible regardless of your location). Moreover, many outdoor spots are still open for visits—zoos, conservation centers, landmarks, battlefields, campgrounds. I've found that planning out one or two diversions a month gives us all something to look forward to.

On a daily basis, you'll probably be hitting four core subjects and one or two electives. Allow me to walk you through some ideas for how to tackle these.[3]

Science

Not a scientist? Me, either. But I've found that while I'm not your best bet to explain the principles of physics, I can prime the pump for more learning later.

You could read through a series on the history of science, or tackle a biography of Archimedes. You could stake off a corner of the back yard and meticulously record every single living thing in a square meter, observe it every day for a week, record the comings and goings of insects and the tracks of tiny squirrel feet, sketch and measure, calculate, research. Plant a garden, watch it grow. Study the science of baking and get busy in the kitchen.

It would probably be smart, if you aren't purchasing a science curriculum, to consult grade-level standards and be sure you're hitting the fundamentals. This is certainly true for high school

---

[3] See a more comprehensive list in Appendix 2.

subjects—biology, physics, and chemistry. Usually for the younger grades, there are a plethora of lavishly illustrated books (and magazines!) on all kinds of subjects that can stretch and challenge your children's scientific imagination.

English and History

I'm a big believer in rolling history, geography, and English into one. Simply choose an era and read the literature associated with it as you study the historical events. For example, with your high schoolers, find a great history of World War II, one with lots of glossy photos. Simultaneously read Anne Frank and Elie Wiesel. Or dive into Greek mythology with your second-grader as you study Alexander the Great.

Paint maps of the places you study. Compare the political borders of nations at different moments in history. Consider how ancient people mapped the world compared to realistic maps of today. Start a giant timeline, and add to it as you go, pasting up photos of the places and people involved.

Look up the artists and composers of the era you're studying, or if the show tunes of the day haven't been preserved, look up the archaeological discoveries associated with that period. You can almost always find novels about a given epoch as well as works actually written at the time, and I can almost guarantee that there's an age-appropriate book corresponding to every corner of the world.

Librarians are your friends.

Most years, I have purchased a literature-based curriculum to simplify my decision-making around what to teach in the liberal arts department. But this is not entirely necessary. It's likely that your local school follows a historical arc year by year, alternating between world history and American history, for example. Finding out what 5th graders usually cover in your district requires only asking the question; you might even be able to get a copy of the public school syllabus and follow along. You don't have to hit every bullet point on the list, but it might comfort you to know that Lily read all about the Revolutionary War and memorized the Preamble of the Declaration if that's indeed what she was going to do in Ms. Nelson's class this year.

After a good, long soak in the history of a period, you'll want to get your kids writing. Create a newspaper set in the antebellum South. Write an editorial about global warming. Pen a Shakespearean-style sonnet. Write a time-traveling story that hops over to ancient Rome. Pretend that you are Anne Boleyn, and imagine the diary she would have kept after marrying Henry VIII. Write a mini-biography of Napoleon. Your entire spelling and grammar curriculum can grow out of the editing process as you check your child's work. "See that kids that's what we call a run-on sentence don't do that anymore."

There are a number of surprisingly fun, easily readable books on grammar—not workbooks, mind you, although there are plenty of workbooks on the market if Billy needs extra practice. Spelling and vocabulary are easily culled from any given book your child is reading. Just flip through the book and make a list, then have your kiddo look them up, copy a definition, learn the spelling. Easy peasy. Copy work, too, is a valuable writing tool: have the child copy a gem of a sentence from their daily reading and discuss for a minute how the sentence works. Extra points for legible handwriting.

For my own children, I like to divvy up our history/language work into chunks—15 minutes to free-write in a journal (or sometimes to respond to what they've just read), 30 minutes to read a chapter of history aloud with Mom, 45 minutes to read a novel silently, 30 minutes to work on an application assignment. Just that amount of work will fill two hours without breaking a sweat.

Math

There are practice quizzes and number games out the wazoo, flash cards and dice, counting cubes and puzzles. But there's really no good substitute for a strong, comprehensive math curriculum. Don't remember how to graph a quadratic equation? No worries. You don't need to be a math scholar in order for your child to stay afloat. There are DVD-based math courses and online math emporiums galore. There are tutors, teachers, and online schools you can sign up for. If you are numerically inclined, you can easily buy a textbook and the accompanying teacher's guide; for the younger grades in particular, most of us could sufficiently explain the concepts to squeak by. (When you get stuck, Google your question, and chances are, a video will pop up to explain it away.)

If you hate math with a fiery passion (ahem), it's not too hard to find a way to outsource your algebraic headache.

Once you've picked your poison, math class is simple. You do it. Every day. You do a quiz every other week or so and make sure everyone understands how to work the problems. And whenever possible, especially for younger kids, use tangible objects to count, measure, multiply, and divide. Find a fun math channel on the internet and watch supplemental explanatory videos if that helps things to click.

Foreign Language

Like math, foreign language study is very cut-and-dried. You either conjugated the verb correctly, or you didn't. However, Mandarin Chinese isn't something you can teach proficiently if you haven't mastered the subject. If you happen to be bilingual, this is your moment! Grab that skill and a handy textbook and go to town. If you speak only English, this is another subject to outsource. Beginners can easily spend a year working through something like Rosetta Stone, but if your child was scheduled to tackle third year Latin, you might want to consider an online course to fill in the gap.

For elementary learners, though, a foreign language might be fun to explore together, hobby-style. You could use an app like Duolingo or watch PBS kids' shows in Spanish, with English subtitles. Remember, at this age, it's just an elective, and missing a year of intensive study won't ruin your kids' linguistic ambitions.

Art, Music, Drama

Never has any subject been easier to explore or more delightful to attempt than artistic work of any kind: painting, photography, music, drama, dance. The whole purpose of the arts is creative personal expression, and you don't have to be Mozart to have fun with these. Keep in mind that if your child is seriously pursuing an artistic hobby (weekly piano lessons, perhaps, or ballet class), this work can certainly be counted as part of your school day. For the rest of us dabblers, the arts are a sort of pressure-release valve that can breathe joy into the humdrum.

While it's admirable for everyone to sample all sorts of artsy activities, it's a shame when a recalcitrant child is forced to participate in an activity he or she loathes. That just ruins it for everyone. But perhaps there is a latent artistic yearning in your young one: a deep desire to throw pots, for instance, or a fascination with movie soundtracks. Giving your kids time to chase these wild hares is a gift for them, an opportunity for something special to blossom.

Art is never a waste of time. As Dostoevsky said, "beauty will save the world." In our hurry-scurry, rat-race life, we're quickly losing our creativity. Find ways to inject creative space into your kids' days, and they will thank you for it.

* * *

What will The Learner Be Able To *Do*? Hmm. How about this instead:

The Learner Will Want to Know More.

William Butler Yeats said, "Education is not the filling of a pail, but the lighting of a fire." College isn't the goal. Career isn't the goal. And education is not a necessary evil. It is one of the great inspirations of the world, a game-changing gift that we often take for granted.

Consider: your kids have been given a quarter of a lifetime to revel in the collected discoveries of the world's best thinkers. Very little is required of them: no physical labor, no quota of production. Others work so that they can use the most strategic season of their developing mind to drink it all in.

Why do lightning bugs shine? Where did we get words like dawdle, cattywampus, filibuster? Who invented automobiles?

We read and memorize and recite the strange magic of Shakespeare and Annie Dillard, thrill to the wild stories of Genghis Khan and David Livingstone. We listen in to the Big Ideas of Plato, Luther, Edison; try to get our heads around the words of Jesus; hear the sad tales of glory-hounding humans from Nero to Hitler gone amok. We ask,

How can we prevent atrocities? What marvels are left to discover? What corners of the globe are bucket-listable? Can even small people like me change the world?

May this year—this strange, unexpected year, be an opportunity that we seize—not to fill a pail, but to light a fire. What fun it could be.

A Few Academic Nuts and Bolts: Legalese and Student Assessment

Homeschool laws vary by state, and you certainly need to look into any legally mandated requirements in your area. Check out the Homeschool Legal Defense Association's website for state-by-state guidelines. If you are simply facilitating online school as mandated by your district, you should already be in compliance with these rules; just be sure to follow whatever your school is asking you to do. But if you have decided to take a break from the public school curriculum of your district, you will need to be sure you obey the laws of your state.

Oftentimes, you will be asked to keep a careful record of what schooling actually took place. But it may or may not be expected that you offer regular comprehension tests. In our area, odd-numbered grades must take a national placement test to ensure that they are staying on track. I leave it to you to learn what is necessary in your area.

Philosophically, there are many schools of thought on student assessment. I appreciate the quick ability to gauge from an end-of-unit test whether or not my kids have mastered the material, but there is more than one way to accomplish this. Daily, oral Q&A works well for our family: *Why did such-and-such happen? How are these two things different? Tell me how you would measure X, Y, and Z.* Writing assignments that demonstrate comprehension work well; having a child teach something to a sibling is great. For some subjects, memorization is the only way to go, and in those instances a quiz might be simplest.

4.

LEANING IN

Back in 2001, Marcus Buckingham and Donald O. Clifton co-authored a book called *Now, Discover Your Strengths*, one of the top ten bestselling business books of all time. The ministry team that I was part of at the time used the "Strengths Finder" test to explore our various personalities. Many fascinating conversations ensued. The premise of the book is that spending all of our time whittling away our weaknesses is a wrongheaded approach that will get you nowhere fast. Far better, the authors argue, to discover, maximize, and operate out of your strengths. Not necessarily your abilities, they would hasten to say, but your passions. What do you love to do? Do that.

Buckingham explains that to lean into your strengths is to live according to who you truly are, taking seriously who you were made to be (in order to contribute your gifts to the world). He points out that even on a neurological level we have the most potential for brain growth in areas of pre-existing strength.[4]

I think there's a great application for this in the world of education.

Imagine Shakespeare as a child. Historically, we know that there was a strong local grammar school in Stratford-upon-Avon, Shakespeare's home town, where in all likelihood young Will spent many long days. The school concentrated on just a few things, namely, Latin and Greek. For a language lover like Shakespeare, the deep dive into grammar, rhetoric, and philosophical classics was a natural fit. Later, we find that his plays are peppered with allusions to classical works, drawing on a lifelong sourcebook of material. But what if Shakespeare had been sent to a

---

[4] https://www.marcusbuckingham.com/rwtb/invest-in-your-strengths-2/

STEM school today, spending the vast majority of his time on math, science, and technology?

On the other hand, what if Einstein had attended Shakespeare's school, and never had a math lesson at all? What a tragedy that would have been!

What an opportunity we have to craft the perfect education for our kids this year, taking into account each child's unique makeup. If your quirky kiddo doesn't neatly fit into the mold of a bigger classroom, here's a chance to tailor a special mold just for her.

You have a year stretching out before you in which to play to your child's strengths. Is he fascinated by insects and bored to tears by poetry? Completely incapable of legible cursive but quick at calculations? Unable to sit still for thirty minutes but with the impassioned imagination of Tolkein?

What if, this year, you let him just… be? Let him excel still more at the thing which makes his heart sing. Let him read an extra hour of history because he loves it instead of squeezing in extra practice in the periodic table.

Do you have a night owl? Then why pry her out of bed early? Let her sleep. You can adjust your schedule to work with your family's rhythm. There's plenty of time.

Do you have a fidgety artistic kid? Then let her draw while you read out loud, and siphon off some of that nervous energy.

This year could be almost a sabbatical for your children, an extended oasis in the middle of their academic career. There will definitely be times you have to gut it out through the worst kind of drudgery, but the more time you can devote to what makes your child uniquely special, the smoother your days will be, and the more refreshing this pause in the daily hustle.

And parents? Play to your own strengths, too. I say to you now as a literature lover, if you hate Robert Frost, then by all means do not teach Robert Frost to your children! At the end of the day, you'll both hate Robert Frost, and that's a crime against humanity. When it comes time to wax poetical, let your kids hear from someone who really loves poetry. The kids may not like it any more than you do, but at least they got a fair shot.

(Knowing my own disastrous relationship with math, I no longer even attempt to teach it. The best thing I can do is help my kids figure out where to direct their questions, point them to solid resources, and get out of the way. Online classes? Well worth my money, every penny.)

If you are fortunate to live in a robust community, you may find it helpful to try this homeschool experiment together with other families. I know a group of parents who gather every week and trade subjects. One dad leads out in science experiments, another mom teaches writing. One day out of seven, the kids are together, learning from an expert. The rest of the week, they stay on pace in a textbook, but Wednesdays? Wednesdays they get to break routine. You might be able to work out a similar arrangement with a long-distance friend via Zoom or Skype.

Leaning into your strengths also means leaning into the joy of teaching, the joy, for your kids, of learning.

It's not terribly hard to start the school year well. Week one, you can usually find a sharp pencil when you need one, you usually get up when the sun rises and have a decent breakfast. Week two, things can start to get a little wobbly. The book's gone missing. The dog ate my homework.

What would it take to still have enthusiasm and a merry heart come, say, January? What can prevent burnout and a trip to the funny farm?

Leaning into your strengths is pretty key. To do most often what you do best, to do most frequently what you love, this means that the high percentage of your time is given to something joyful. It sounds so Pollyanna until you realize that the opposite is demonstrably true. To spend most of your day doing what you like least is to set yourself up for misery; children who hate school rarely succeed there.

Another key for long-lasting happiness in the homeschool life is gratitude. Remembering that life is short (and a worldwide pandemic has a helpful way of reminding us) gives urgency to our relationships, and thankfulness for what we have. Remembering that these days are fleeting makes the irritations shrink into proportion.

Proverbs 14:4 says (curiously): "Where there are no oxen, the manger is clean." Come again? We might say, "where there are no children, the house stays tidy." The messes, the frustrations, the hyperactivity, the noise—all of these are reminders of the presence of an amazing blessing, a family.

Perhaps the homeschool journey you're embarking on is a one-off. Just this year, just until things go back to normal. All the more reason to enjoy it while you can—it won't last forever.

Or perhaps you will come to the end of the school year and find that you don't want to go back to normal. You like the new normal, in spite of the fact it was a bit of a surprise. You want to homeschool *forever*! Even so, it won't last long.

The average human lifespan is a short 30,000 days. How many days have you already completed? Psalm 103 says,

> As for man, his days are like grass;
>   he flourishes like a flower of the field;
> for the wind passes over it, and it is gone,
>   and its place knows it no more. (Psalm 103:15-16)

Our days on earth are a short burst of beauty; our kids "grow like a weed." This is actually good news; our lives here (full of messes and heartbreaks and brokenness) are just the prelude to an eternity of purpose, joy, and fulfillment. But it does mean that this year is precious. These 365 days will come and go before you know it.

Lean in.

Enjoy it while you can.

5.

A FEW FINAL WORDS OF ENCOURAGEMENT

I think what Jerry Seinfeld said about two-year-olds equally applies to homeschool. It's "kind of like having a blender, but you don't have a top for it."

There will be messes. Mistakes. Discouraging days. Laughter. There will be Eureka moments of great discovery and eye-twitching moments of great drudgery. Some days you will suggest a game of hide and seek just so you can hide from the short people. Some days will seem so absolutely perfect that no one will even realize you were actually doing school (like sneaking spinach into a smoothie to get some vitamins in). One day, your teenager might actually rest a head on your shoulder and say thanks.

The days are short; the world is spinning fast. If I bore the responsibility of figuring it all out, I would be doomed. But I don't.

Your children are part of a bigger story, and their part in it is not yet clear. But it will be. All of my own (*breathtaking*) mistakes have been redeemed for good, even if I couldn't see it at the time. All your kids' struggles, wanderings, procrastination, failures, slugging it out through boredom, triumphing over disaster—all of it is part of a bigger plan, aimed at their sanctification, resilience, and fortitude.

One of my all-time favorite Psalms speaks beautifully to our good Father's meticulous attention to detail in each individual's life. May I suggest, take a moment and pray it through, once for yourself, and another time over your children. Turn David's reflection into your own, and draw strength from it.

Psalm 139

1 O Lord, you have searched me and known me!
2 You know when I sit down and when I rise up;
   you discern my thoughts from afar.
3 You search out my path and my lying down
   and are acquainted with all my ways.
4 Even before a word is on my tongue,

behold, O Lord, you know it altogether.
5 You hem me in, behind and before,
and lay your hand upon me.
6 Such knowledge is too wonderful for me;
it is high; I cannot attain it.
7 Where shall I go from your Spirit?
Or where shall I flee from your presence?
8 If I ascend to heaven, you are there!
If I make my bed in Sheol, you are there!
9 If I take the wings of the morning
and dwell in the uttermost parts of the sea,
10 even there your hand shall lead me,
and your right hand shall hold me.
11 If I say, "Surely the darkness shall cover me,
and the light about me be night,"
12 even the darkness is not dark to you;
the night is bright as the day,
for darkness is as light with you.
13 For you formed my inward parts;
you knitted me together in my mother's womb.
14 I praise you, for I am fearfully and wonderfully made.
Wonderful are your works;
my soul knows it very well.
15 My frame was not hidden from you,
when I was being made in secret,
intricately woven in the depths of the earth.
16 Your eyes saw my unformed substance;
in your book were written, every one of them,
the days that were formed for me,
when as yet there was none of them.
17 How precious to me are your thoughts, O God!
How vast is the sum of them!
18 If I would count them, they are more than the sand.

> I awake, and I am still with you….
> 23 Search me, O God, and know my heart!
>   Try me and know my thoughts!
> 24 And see if there be any grievous way in me,
>   and lead me in the way everlasting!

Sometimes I just need a reminder that God's got this. None of my scurrying, worrying, or striving will help matters along. God's plan for my kids isn't contingent upon my great wisdom; the Father who can pluck a shepherd off the hillside and set him upon a throne can certainly take my messy, imperfect love, and my kids' talents and passions, and create of it all a beautiful life.

When fear rises, look to love. Jesus' love is big enough to catch you; his perfect love "casts out fear" (I John 4:18). When doubts assail you, lift your eyes to him. His steadfast love is never-changing. When stress has you feeling frazzled, breathe deep, and choose to be thankful. When the days feel everlasting, remember that they are, in reality, short. When you realize that you aren't enough, remember that he is.

Accept this year as a gift. As James puts it, "Every good and perfect gift is from above, coming down from the Father of lights with whom there is

no variation or shadow due to change" (James 1:17).
If it's a gift, it's an opportunity for joy. If it's part of
God's plan, it will work together for good. As
William Cowper put it, "Ye fearful saints, fresh
courage take; The clouds you so much dread, are big
with mercy and shall break in blessings on your head."

APPENDIX A:

FAMILY AIM-FOR-IT BIBLE VERSES, FAMILY COVENANT, & SCREEN TIME RULES

Bible Verses

I Corinthians 13: 4-8

"Love is patient and kind; love does not envy or boast; it is not arrogant or rude. It does not insist on its own way; it is not irritable or resentful; it does not rejoice at wrongdoing, but rejoices with the truth. Love bears all things, believes all things, hopes all things, endures all things. Love never ends."

Ephesians 5:1-2

"Therefore be imitators of God, as beloved children. And walk in love, as Christ loved us and gave himself up for us, a fragrant offering and sacrifice to God."

Matthew 5:1-16

"Seeing the crowds, he went up on the mountain, and when he sat down, his disciples came to him. And he opened his mouth and taught them, saying:

'Blessed are the poor in spirit, for theirs is the kingdom of heaven.

'Blessed are those who mourn, for they shall be comforted.

'Blessed are the meek, for they shall inherit the earth.

'Blessed are those who hunger and thirst for righteousness, for they shall be satisfied.

'Blessed are the merciful, for they shall receive mercy.

'Blessed are the pure in heart, for they shall see God.

'Blessed are the peacemakers, for they shall be called sons of God.

'Blessed are those who are persecuted for righteousness' sake, for theirs is the kingdom of heaven.

'Blessed are you when others revile you and persecute you and utter all kinds of evil against you falsely on my account. Rejoice and be glad, for your reward is great in heaven, for so they persecuted the prophets who were before you.

'You are the salt of the earth, but if salt has lost its taste, how shall its saltiness be restored? It is no longer good for anything except to be thrown out and trampled under people's feet.

'You are the light of the world. A city set on a hill cannot be hidden. Nor do people light a lamp and put it under a basket, but on a stand, and it gives light to all in the house. In the same way, let your light shine before others, so that they may see your good works and give glory to your Father who is in heaven.'"

II Peter 1:5-10

"For this very reason, make every effort to supplement your faith with virtue, and virtue with knowledge, and knowledge with self-control, and self-control with steadfastness, and steadfastness with godliness, and godliness with brotherly affection, and brotherly affection with love. For if these qualities are yours and are increasing, they keep you from being ineffective or unfruitful in the knowledge of our Lord Jesus Christ. For whoever lacks these qualities is so nearsighted that he is blind, having forgotten that he was cleansed from his former sins. Therefore, brothers, be all the more diligent to confirm your calling and election, for if you practice these qualities you will never fall."

I John 2:15-17

"Do not love the world or the things in the world. If anyone loves the world, the love of the Father is not in him. For all that is in the world—the desires of the flesh and the desires of the eyes and pride of life—is not from the Father but is from the world. And the world is passing away along with its desires, but whoever does the will of God abides forever."

I John 4:7-8, 20

"Beloved, let us love one another, for love is from God, and whoever loves has been born of God and knows God. Anyone who does not love does not know God, because God is love....If anyone says, 'I love God,' and hates his brother, he is a liar; for he who does not love his brother whom he has seen cannot love God whom he has not seen."

Family Covenant

Because it is our family's highest priority to glorify God by enjoying Him together, we commit to strive towards the following ideals out of love for Jesus and each other:

Grace

- We recognize that we are forgiven, so we will extend forgiveness.
- We will try hard to keep no record of wrongs.
- We will make every effort to be kind.
- We know that we have been given much more than we deserve, and we will not demand our "rights."

Gratitude

- We will actively count our blessings.
- We will verbally express thankfulness.
- We won't whine, complain, or grumble. Instead we will encourage, rejoice, pitch in, and be cheerful.

Humility

- We will consider others better than ourselves, and seek to outdo one another in love.

- We will look for ways to serve one another.

- In our house we will not worry about the opinion of others, but only seek to please God.

Unselfishness

- Our gratitude will overflow in generosity as we put others first. We will share, take turns, and refuse to be greedy with our time and money.

- We will work hard not to make more work for others. If we get it out, we'll put it away. If we get it dirty, we'll clean it up. If we borrow it, we'll return it.

Purity

- We do not welcome the pollution of the world in our home. Like Job, we covenant to set no vile thing before our eyes.

- If we see something inappropriate, we will turn away, and take steps to prevent seeing it again.

- We will not keep secrets out of shame, but confess our struggles to one another, welcome accountability, and bring everything into the light.

Responsibility

- We agree to function as a team, each with our own strengths, roles and responsibilities.

- We recognize that we must finish what we start, work diligently and with excellence at our tasks, and not shirk our duties in laziness.

- We will approach our work with a sense of honor, not half-heartedly; with optimism, not dread; and with a merry heart, not a grumpy spirit.

Integrity

- We will always tell the truth.

- We will be true to our word and do what we promise.

- We will accept consequences without seeking to justify our sin.

- We will obey.

Joy

- We will do our best to have fun, lighten one another's loads, affirm one another, and laugh often.

- We will happily join in games, family outings, social events, outdoor recreation, trips, and holiday activities, making our own traditions as we go and creating our own zany family culture.

- We will happily participate in family prayer time or devotions and point each other to Jesus however we can.

Screen Time Rules

Because computers and other forms of entertainment technology can become so addictive and so isolating, we agree to the following rules in order to keep screen time in check:

- Family time takes priority over screen time (including phones, tablets, computers, TV, etc.).

- Outside of school or work, I agree not to spend more than two hours per day alone in front of a screen. This includes surfing the internet, watching a show, playing a game, Garage Band, Skype, email, etc.

- I will not use the internet alone behind closed doors (for instance, alone in my room at bedtime).

- I will not bring devices to the dinner table or family outings.

- I will not wear headphones in the car (except sometimes on road trips).

- I will not post photos or videos without permission.

- I will never post personal information (address, birthday, contact information) on a public forum.

- I will not develop online friendships with strangers. If a stranger reaches out and I would like to chat, I will ask first. I promise to alert my parents if I receive inappropriate or alarming communication from anyone.

- I agree that screen time is a privilege that may be revoked, reduced, or suspended as a consequence or simply to prioritize other things.

- Schoolwork and chores will come before screen time. If a parent needs my help or involvement in any way, I will pause whatever I was doing without complaint.

- I agree not to hog family devices or borrow equipment without asking.

- I will take care of my own devices—being careful where I put them, how I carry them, how I operate them, and being careful not to waste energy or resources.

- I will use good etiquette (for example, turning off noisy notifications in public or turning off my device to engage in conversation). I will follow rules external to our house (no texting while driving, no internet during class).

- I understand that disregarding these rules will result in my devices being taken away or my privileges being suspended.

APPENDIX B:

INTEGRATING SUBJECTS AND OUTSIDE-THE-BOX IDEAS

Following is a list of a few favorite homeschooling books and activities by category and (very roughly) by age group. There are a million more, and a few hours on the internet can yield a plethora of suggestions. (When I say "middle grades," I'm considering a broad category of kids from maybe 4th grade through 8th. When I say "elementary," I'm thinking kindergarten through 3rd.)

A helpful resource for all things homeschool is the Caffy Duffy review site: *https://cathyduffyreviews.com/#*. There is also a specific homeschooling section on Christianbook that can point you not only to specific resources, but to publishers that specialize in homeschooling, like Abeka (video-based) or Apologia (mostly science).

You can find math-only video courses, handwriting help, and more in this one-stop-shop: *https://www.christianbook.com/page/homeschool*.

In addition, there are a number of reputable online schools, many in the classical education camp, which can do all of the teaching for you, but they tend to be pricey. One that we've liked is Wilson Hill Academy. Read parent reviews to get a sense for the tone and vibe of various institutions if you want to go that route.

Finally, I recommend Sonlight, which our family has used for years. Many of the fantastic books I'm listing below are resources we discovered through Sonlight's curriculum collection. If you hate the idea of picking and choosing which books to read, Sonlight's got you covered: you can purchase a year-long curriculum from them that helps to pace out a prescribed list of books: *https://www.sonlight.com*.

Science Overview

I highly recommend the Usborne Books collection. Lavishly photographed, encyclopedic, geared for every age level. There are internet links in many of their titles, with corresponding videos for further exploration. Several of their activity books contain a year's worth of elementary-level science experiments, with all of the necessary instructions for do-it-yourself lab work.

The DK Eyewitness books are also great for going deep on any given subject.

A fun nature activity that can be done wherever you live is to pick up a book on the wildlife in your area (for example, *On The Trail of Colorado Critters* or *The Backyard Bug Book for Kids*) and a second book like *Tracks, Scats, and Signs* and head out to the nearest nature trail. Even a city park would do. Then engage your kids in a scavenger hunt, looking for evidence of lions and tigers and bears. (Oh my!)

Other science-related activity ideas: visit the zoo, stop by the aquarium, go on a camping trip, look for crawdads, visit an air and space museum, visit the airport, tour a botanic garden, check out a butterfly museum, go fishing, take up rock collecting, plant a garden, investigate baking, visit a working farm, study bird calls or go bird watching.

By the by, a quick search for "home science experiments for kids" on Amazon yielded page after page of books devoted to easy experiments you can do in your kitchen. And Hobby Lobby often carries lab kits, robotics projects, and crafty science activities.

Science: Middle Grades

Alex Frith, *What's Science All About?*

This is also an Usborne book. Great intro to biology, chemistry, and physics. Well-written, engaging, thorough. Perfect to set the stage for high school science.

Ronald and Peg Marson, *TOPS Learning System #39: Green Thumbs: Corn and Beans*

Simply reading this book would be the ultimate snooze fest, but doing the activities (time consuming, but totally worth it) made for a great semester of science. Designed for grades 4-12.

Integrating Science and Literature: Elementary/Middle Grades

J. Patrick Lewis, editor, *National Geographic Book of Nature Poetry: More than 200 Poems With Photographs That Float, Zoom, and Bloom!*

The title is pretty self-explanatory, but the combo of beautiful photography, classic poetry, and attention to nature is a great bridge between science and the arts.

Integrating Science and Literature: High School

Wendell Berry, *This Day: Collected and New Sabbath Poems*

Beautiful reflections on nature, among other subjects.

Annie Dillard, *Pilgrim at Tinker Creek*

One of the great American works of narrative non-fiction, this Pulitzer prize winner is a startling, sometimes troubling, always fascinating examination of faith and science, told with some of the best prose you'll find in English.

Henry David Thoreau, *Walden*

History Overview

We have found that using one long history book to guide us over the length of the year works well, supplemented by lots of shorter books that examine a given subject in greater detail. The DK Eyewitness and Usborne collections are great for shorter history books as well as science.

Some history-related activities: pan for gold, do crayon rubbings of historical markers or gravestones; visit the nearest landmark, archaeological site, or ghost town; build a replica of a famous building; dress as historical characters for a costume party; watch a historical movie or play; recreate a historical craft (like weaving); or make (and eat) an authentic meal.

Susan Wise Bauer, *The Story of the World* series

Especially great for middle grades. I liked to use the audio version and help the kids take notes, jotting down key people, places, and events. Good practice for listening to lectures.

Joy Hakim, *A History of US*

My daughter read through this 11-book series over a whole school year (intense). My son did three a year through middle school. (Much better.) Very engaging.

Virgil Hillyer, *A Child's History of the World*

Great to read aloud with younger kids.

The World Wars

From our friends at Usborne, is a great dive into this period. Could work for middle or high school.

Integrating History and Science

Here are two subjects that mesh surprisingly well. After all, scientific discoveries often have huge, culture-shaping impact. In addition to the books I've listed below (mostly for middle and upper grades), tap into your local or state history. Much of it is tied to the scientific or technological achievements of people who lived in your area. For example, you may be able to visit a Native American site to learn about farming techniques, a seaport with exhibits related to nautical history, or an old-fashioned railroad where you could study trains.

Integrating History and Science: Middle Grades

Jeanne Bendick, *Archimedes and the Door of Science*

A fun biography that merges history and science. Upper elementary or middle school.

Noah Blake and Eric Sloane, *Diary of an Early American Boy*

I looked forward to reading this to my kids every day, as I found it completely fascinating. Noah Blake's diary from 1805, describing (with great illustrations) the improvised technology of a New England farm.

Jacqueline Fortey, *DK Eyewitness Books: Great Scientists: Discover the Pioneers Who Changed the Way We Think About Our World*

Margot Lee Shetterly, *Hidden Figures: Young Readers' Edition*

As retold in the movie of the same title (There is also an adult version of this book.)

Integrating History and Science: High School

Bill Bryson, *A Short History of Nearly Everything*

Not from a faith-based perspective, but an engaging conversation-starter.

Joy Hakim, *The Story of Science* **series**

You'll come away with a deeper understanding of science as well as the history of thought and the impact of scientific discovery on the larger world. There is a companion series of workbooks, as well.

David McCullough, *The Wright Brothers*

Also available in audiobook form.

Integrating History and Literature

We have studied these two subjects together for so long I can't imagine studying them separately. Almost any historical event you'd like to study with your kids is the subject of a novel, a poem, or a play.

> "Listen my children and you will hear / Of the midnight ride of Paul Revere…"

That's just the tip of the iceberg.

Traveling? There are 57 National Historical Parks in the American national park system, most of which have a gift shop attached. Visit any one of them and you can pick up books to extend your learning.

In early elementary school, you can certainly laugh along with *Green Eggs and Ham*, but you could just as easily read *Long, Tall Lincoln*. Check out scholastic.com (the "if you..." series is quite well-done) or look on schoolspecialty.com to find historical fiction sets for every grade level.

Integrating History and Literature: Middle Grades

Laurie Halse Anderson, *Chains*

An enslaved young girl spies to help others win freedom in the Revolutionary War.

Gary Blackwood, *The Shakespeare Stealer*

Great for Elizabethan England and an intro to Shakespeare.

Esther Forbes, *Johnny Tremain*

Revolutionary War story ruined by Disney.

Marguerite Henry, *Justin Morgan Had a Horse*

Or *Misty of Chincoteague*, or *King of the Wind*. All great horse stories, but *Justin Morgan* highlights the historical moment in colonial Vermont very well.

Irene Hunt, *Across Five Aprils*

Civil War story for middle schoolers.

Jean Lathan, *Carry On, Mr. Bowditch*

Story of an 18th-century sailor and inventor.

Lois Lowry, *Number the Stars.*

On the Holocaust.

Patricia MacLachlan, *Sarah, Plain and Tall.*

Takes place on the American frontier.

Carolyn Meyer, *Mary, Bloody Mary*

The story of Mary Tudor.

Rick Riordan, *The Lightning Thief*

Great to pair with Greek mythology and the ancient world.

Elizabeth George Speare, *The Sign of the Beaver*

Captivating story about pioneering colonists in Maine.

Elizabeth Speare, *The Witch of Blackbird Pond*

Leads to some fairly sophisticated conversations about religious freedom in colonial America.

Mildred Taylor, *Roll of Thunder, Hear My Cry*

Challenging subject matter (racism and Jim Crow era history) but great for developing empathy.

Laura Ingalls Wilder, *Little House on the Prairie* **series**

Integrating History and Literature: High School

James Fenimore Cooper, *The Last of the Mohicans*

Set during the French and Indian War.

Steven Crane, *The Red Badge of Courage*

A quick Civil War classic.

Charles Dickens, *A Tale of Two Cities*

Vive la France!

Anthony Doerr, *All the Light We Cannot See*

Warning: most of this book, though dealing with a difficult subject, is fairly PG. But near the end of the book there are a few scenes you might want to preview before you hand it to even your older kids. It's a great exploration of the mind of a German soldier during World War II.

Fitzgerald, F. Scott Fitzgerald, *The Great Gatsby*

Flapper era, unreliable narrator, whom can you trust?

Anne Frank, The Diary of a Young Girl: The Definitive Edition

World War II.

Nathaniel Hawthorne, *The Scarlet Letter*

Puritans, guilt, revenge.

Ernest Hemingway, *A Farewell to Arms*

World War II romance and hopelessness.

Victor Hugo, *Les Miserables*

It's a long one, folks.

Arthur Miller, *The Crucible*

A play about the Salem Witch trials.

Harriet Beecher Stowe, *Uncle Tom's Cabin*

When Abraham Lincoln met Stowe, he reportedly said, "So this is the little lady who made this big war."

Corrie ten Boom, *The Hiding Place*

Perfect to accompany World War II history.

Louis Zamperini, *Devil at My Heels: A Heroic Olympian's Astonishing Story Of Survival As A Japanese Pow In World War II*

The autobiography of Zamperini, better known from Laura Hildebrand's *Unbroken*. In his own words, including his conversion to Christianity and testimony of what happened next.

I have heard great things about many other books for the high school age group, but not having read them myself I am cautious to recommend them. A few to consider: *Code Talker: The First and Only Memoir By One of the Original Navajo Code Talkers of WWII* by Chester Nez; *The Immortal Life of Henrietta Lacks*, by Rebecca Skloot, and *The Boys in the Boat: Nine Americans and Their Epic Quest for Gold at the 1936 Berlin Olympics,* by Daniel James Brown.

Integrating History and Faith

No matter how old your kids are—and whether you homeschool or not— reading gripping stories of Christian heroes together as a family is a challenging, faith-building activity. A great bedtime or after dinner routine, this is a habit I hope will outlast the suddenly schooling season.

Integrating History and Faith: Elementary

Window on the World

This is a lavishly photographed, kid-friendly book that walks through one people group at a time. It's perfect for geography; be sure to pull out a globe and locate every country under discussion. Do we really believe our kids' prayers make a difference? Then this book is a world-changer.

Neil Anderson, *In Search of the Source.*

One of our favorite family read-alouds, this is an often hilarious true story of a Bible translator's work.

Irene Howat, *Ten Boys/Girls* **series**

With titles like "Ten Boys Who Changed the World" and "Ten Girls Who Didn't Give In," these are great true stories at the intersection of history and faith.

Integrating History and Faith: Middle Grades

The Torchlighter DVDs are 30-minute true stories about martyrs, missionaries, and heroes. Usually someone dies, tragically (which is why I listed it for older kids), but always the stories focus on God's powerful work through individuals fully committed to Him. Our favorite is the Gladys Aylward story, about an indomitable little lady who brought the gospel to a Chinese village, rescuing over 100 orphans along the way.

Geoff & Janet Benge, *Christian Heroes* series

One of my personal favorites is the biography of George Müller, who, without asking anyone for funding, was able to begin a series of orphanages in 19th-century England.

John Hendrix, *The Faithful Spy: Dietrich Bonhoeffer and the Plot to Kill Hitler.*

A graphic novel rendition of the life of Bonhoeffer, the theologian and would-be assassin of Hitler.

Integrating History and Faith: High School

E. Michael and Sharon O. Rusten, *The One Year Book of Christian History*

A great add-on to go with longer books, and a quick read at a page per day. You'll get a good sampling of stories that span the last 2,000 years of church history.

Randy Alcorn, *Safely Home*

This gripping novel about faith in communist China is brought to you by the author of such theological heavy-weights as *Heaven* and *Happiness*.

Brother Andrew, *God's Smuggler*

A riveting missionary biography set in the 20th century. "Brother Andrew," as he is called, smuggles Bibles behind the Iron Curtain.

C.S. Lewis, *The Screwtape Letters*

Amusing and thought-provoking letters from one demon to another. Great for discussion of spiritual warfare.

Faith, PS

If you haven't been in the habit of daily family devotionals, this could be a great time to start! One resource I recommend is *Family Time Hymns: Experiencing Timeless Truth Through Music*, by Jenna Hallock. Designed for whole families (multiple age levels) to enjoy together, this is a book that will help you unpack classic hymns and mine them for treasure.

Art and Other Subjects

One suggestion is to make a habit of Googling the artwork or music connected to any time period or place you may be studying. Lots of artists have expressed their outrage at current events with a paintbrush: Picasso, for example, and his groundbreaking *Guernica*. Or take Tchaikovsky, whose 1812 Overture commemorated the defeat of Napoleon.

Then there have been artist/inventors, like daVinci (Italy/the Renaissance/classical painting/history of flight/history of war machines… you can definitely spend some time on this guy. It is even possible to buy model kits of daVinci's inventions, which makes for a fun project.) A trip to a local art exhibit would be the icing on the cake.

There have been artist/missionaries, like Lilias Trotter, artist/writers, like van Gogh, and artist/scientists like John James Audubon. Many of our historical heroes were gifted in multiple disciplines, like Galileo, Benjamin Franklin, Thomas Jefferson, or Michelangelo. Studying the biographies of people like this alongside some of their artistic achievements brings history to life.

In addition, illustrating science or history or literature is a great way to connect art with other subjects. And of course, a trip to a local art exhibit or concert (online, perhaps?) would be the icing on the cake.

Classics and Excellent Stories: Elementary

Your kids will be transitioning from Dr. Seuss to challenging chapter books between kindergarten and third grade. Use your discretion, but be sure to include read-aloud books that kids can understand before they are able to read them alone. They'll gain astonishing leaps in vocabulary and comprehension during these grades.

Sometimes a very young child will pick up a beloved story you've read aloud with extra incentive to learn to read, a desire that can jumpstart their ability. (In the first grade, our youngest son literally went from Hop on Pop to Harry Potter in a matter of weeks because he wanted to read for himself a book he'd heard read aloud on a car trip.) If you want your kids to be self-feeders, be sure to include some books simply for the delight of reading, with no special agenda.

C.W. Anderson, *Billy and Blaze* **series**

For the horse lover.

Richard Atwater, *Mr. Popper's Penguins*

Hilarity ensues.

James Barrie, *Peter Pan.*

If you've never actually read the book, you'll be surprised by how delightful the prose is. Great for reading aloud.

Carol Brink, *Caddie Woodlawn*

1860s on the Wisconsin frontier.

Beverly Cleary, *Ramona Quimby, Age 8*

All of Ms. Cleary's books are great, but it's hard to beat the Ramona books.

Meindert De Jong, *The Wheel on the School*

A quiet and slow-moving story.

Kate DiCamillo, *The Tale of Despereaux: Being the Story of a Mouse, a Princess, Some Soup, and a Spool of Thread*

One of those times the book is much better than the movie.

Walter Farley, *The Black Stallion* **series**

More for horse lovers.

Ruth Gannett, *My Father's Dragon*

Elmer Elevator's adventure rescuing a baby dragon.

James Herriot, *James Herriot's Treasury for Children: Warm and Joyful Tales by the Author of All Creatures Great and Small*

This was one of my favorite read-alouds.

Astrid Lindgren, *Pippi Longstocking* **series.**

Make them giggle.

Maude Loveless, *Betsy-Tacy* **series**

Sweet stories of friendship.

A.A. Milne, *The House at Pooh Corner*

Makes the children laugh and the adults cry.

Farley Mowat, *Owls in the Family*

Funny stories from a kid with a pair of trouble-making owls for pets.

Gertrude Warner, *The Box-Car Children*

Adventures from an innocent time.

Marjorie Williams, *The Velveteen Rabbit*

Growing up is bittersweet.

E. B. White, *Charlotte's Web* (truly a tear-jerker),
Stuart Little, **or** *Trumpet of the Swan* (quite funny).

Henry Winterfeld, *Detectives in Togas*

A mystery in ancient Rome.

Classics and Excellent Stories:
Middle Grades

A lot of these have fantastic audio book adaptations which are great for car trips. I find that books aimed at this age group are usually entertaining for the whole family.

Natalie Babbitt, *Tuck Everlasting*

What happens if you live forever?

Frank L. Baum, *The Wizard of Oz* **series**

Quite different from the movie.

Frances Hodgson Burnett, *The Secret Garden* or *The Little Princess*

Watch out for a subversive worldview, but a pair of great stories.

Sheila Burnford, *The Incredible Journey*

Well-done animal story.

Natalie Carlson, *The Family Under the Bridge*

Family read-aloud for Christmas. It will make you cry.

Lewis Carroll, *Alice's Adventures in Wonderland*

Roald Dahl, *The BFG, Charlie and the Chocolate Factory,* or *James and the Giant Peach*

Roald Dahl's imagination was born to make kids laugh.

Kate DiCamillo, *The Miraculous Journey of Edward Tulane*

A story of transformation.

Charles Dickens, *A Christmas Carol*

A great intro to Dickens, short, sweet, and familiar, but be aware that the vocabulary level is fairly challenging.

Dorothy Fisher, *Understood Betsy*

An overprotected little girl goes to live with some outside-the-box relations in the country.

Kenneth Grahame, *The Wind in the Willows*

Fantasy, adventure, camaraderie.

H. C. Holling, *Paddle-to-the-Sea.*

When we read this one, we whittled our own canoes, painted them, and launched them down a stream.

Washington Irving, *The Legend of Sleepy Hollow*

Fun, spooky, challenging read.

Rudyard Kipling, *Just So Stories*

Have them write their own explanatory fable.

Madeliene L'Engle, *A Wrinkle in Time.*

Sci-fi fantasy for the middle school set.

C.S. Lewis, *The Chronicles of Narnia*

A younger child could certainly hang in there to hear Narnia read aloud, but these books are so good that you almost want to save them for later.

Hugh Lofting, *The Voyages of Dr. Dolittle*

A veterinarian and his talking animal friends.

George MacDonald, *The Princess and the Goblin*

One of C.S. Lewis's favorite authors.

Lucy Maud Montgomery, *Anne of Green Gables*

Everyone's favorite redhead.

E. Nesbit, *The Railway Children*

Inspired Lewis's magic wardrobe.

Andrew Peterson, *The Wingfeather Saga*

Singer-songwriter-children's author Peterson writes fantasy books that kids and adults can enjoy.

Barbara Robinson, *The Best Christmas Pageant Ever*

Another Christmas cry-er.

Pam Muñoz Ryan, *Echo*

Magical realism meets moments in history.

Kate Seredy, *The Good Master*

Pre-world war Hungary.

Virginia Sorensen, *Miracles on Maple Hill*

A melancholy book, but sweet.

Jonathan Swift, *Gulliver's Travels*

Fairly challenging.

Albert Terhune, *Lad: A Dog*

Also pretty challenging.

J.R.R. Tolkien, *The Hobbit*

Tolkien practically invented a genre here.

Mark Twain, *The Adventures of Tom Sawyer*

So witty. At least worth reading Chapter 2, "The Glorious Whitewasher."

Jules Verne, *Around the World in Eighty Days*

My kids were so excited by the last chapter that my husband had to ask us to pipe down.

N. D. Wilson, *100 Cupboards*

Fantasy series from N.D. Wilson, a great Christian thinker.

Classics and Excellent Stories: High School

Louisa May Alcott, *Little Women*

Jane Austen

Take your pick. *Emma; Pride and Prejudice;* or *Sense and Sensibility* would be a good introduction to Jane.

Ray Bradbury, *The Illustrated Man*

This is an intriguing collection of sci-fi/fantasy short stories.

John Bunyan, *The Pilgrim's Progress*

Discover why it's been a bestseller for a million years.

G. K. Chesterton, *The Best of Father Brown*

Mysteries from the great Catholic apologist and humorist.

Daniel Dafoe, *Robinson Crusoe*

Charles Dickens

Take your pick.

Leif Enger, *Peace Like a River*

Father and kids set out to save outlaw son.

Gilbreth & Carey, *Cheaper By the Dozen*

Controlled chaos in a huge family.

James Herriot, *All Creatures Great and Small*

Stories from an early 20th-century veterinarian in Yorkshire.

Martin Luther King, Jr., *Letter from a Birmingham Jail*

This is a quick must-read.

Lois Lowry, *The Giver*

Interesting to compare with *Animal Farm* for dystopian fiction.

George Orwell, *Animal Farm*

Mary Ann Shaffer, *The Guernsey Literary and Potato Peel Pie Society*

William Shakespeare

Pick one. A few of the more accessible plays include *MacBeth*, *Much Ado About Nothing*, *Julius Caesar*, and *Romeo and Juliet*. There are some helpful editions with copious explanatory notes or even the entire text in modern English alongside the original. Be sure to then watch the play.

Robert Louis Stevenson, *Dr. Jekyll and Mr. Hyde*

J.R.R. Tolkien, *The Lord of the Rings*

Enough said.

Mark Twain, *The Adventures of Huckleberry Finn*

Many schools are eliminating this from standard curriculum because of the incredible racism depicted. But the potential for a great discussion about race, morality, cultural values, and evolving characters might make it worth a read for your student. Be sure to have the hard conversation, though, and don't assume your kids will see things the way you do. In the same vein, try Harper Lee's *To Kill a Mockingbird*.

Lynne Truss, *Eats, Shoots, and Leaves*

A funny book about commas. Seriously.

Elie Wiesel, *Night*

Wiesel's experience of the Holocaust.

Markus Zusak, *The Book Thief*

Skip this one if you are bothered by rough language and difficult subject matter, but a brilliantly creative World War II novel for young adults.

Made in the USA
Columbia, SC
23 August 2020